T0322594

BOND

BEHIND THE SCENES

BOND

BEHIND THE SCENES

mirrorpix

The History Press

First published 2019

The History Press
97 St George's Place
Cheltenham GL50 3QB
www.thehistorypress.co.uk

British Library Cataloguing in Publication Data.
A catalogue record for this book is available from the British Library.

ISBN 978 0 7509 9075 2

Typesetting and origination by The History Press
Printed in Turkey by Imak

INTRODUCTION

BY MARK BEYNON

Cinema reporting has changed beyond recognition since the 1960s. Gone are the days when journalists and photographers had seemingly unfettered access to film sets and stars, and such is the feverish interest in some cinematic franchises today that studios have become far more vigilant when it comes to leaking on-set information. The release of such material, either through trailers or stills, is now so carefully stage-managed that it requires almost military-like planning.

The advent of social media and dedicated online fan forums has only increased the need for such secrecy. This was demonstrated by the fallout from the hacking of Sony Pictures in 2014, which resulted in the production of the twenty-fourth Bond film, *Spectre*, to be thrown into chaos. Scripts and production notes were posted online, resulting in substantial rewrites.

Indeed, since his unveiling as James Bond in 2005, unofficial glimpses of Daniel Craig donning the famous tuxedo have been largely restricted to photos taken by eagle-eyed photographers with long lenses. A far cry from the days when photographers cheerfully congregated around a bed in which Sean Connery and his latest 'Bond girl' posed for pictures. Pivotal scenes, too, were eagerly captured for posterity by the invited press corp. 'Spoilers' were clearly not a thing in the '60s …

Likewise, it is highly unlikely that any future Bondian henchman would be photographed playfully grappling with two young 007 fans today as Harold Sakata (Oddjob) was when *Goldfinger* was being filmed at Stoke Park in 1964. Nor would pensive actresses be pictured smoking before taking part in an audacious stunt as Karin Dor (Helga Brandt) was when filming *You Only Live Twice* at Pinewood in 1966.

In compiling this collection from the Mirrorpix archive, it has been startling to note the shift in availability of behind-the-scenes stills from the Sean Connery era to that of Roger Moore. And by Pierce Brosnan's tenure as 007, only snaps of film premieres and photocalls were permitted to be taken by anyone other than the official production photographer. How fortunate we are, then, that these photographs are still available to us in a collection such as this, giving us mere mortals an uncensored glimpse of what it was really like on the set of a James Bond film back in the early days of the franchise.

➤ Queues outside the London Pavilion cinema, Piccadilly Circus, to see *Dr. No*, the first James Bond film.

AS JAMES BOND
TECHNICOLOR
HAVE A
SPEARMINT
CHEWING
IAN FLEMING'S
DR. NO
THE FIRST
JAMES BOND
FILM!
STARRING
SEAN CONNERY
AS

▲ Sean Connery and Zena Marshall attend the premiere of *Dr. No*.

➤ (And next page) Sean Connery and Daniela Bianchi (Tatiana Romanova) filming the bedroom scene in *From Russia With Love*.

⌃ Sean Connery on the Pinewood set of *Goldfinger* receiving a massage from Margaret Nolan (Dink).

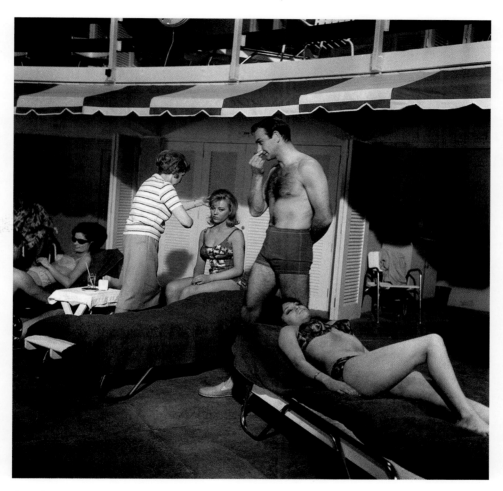

▲ A break in filming as Margaret Nolan has her hair fixed.

▲ Shirley Eaton (Jill Masterson) has gold paint applied to her as Sean Connery looks on.

34 BOND

▲ (And following pages) Sean Connery and Honor Blackman filming their famous love scene in the barn.

▲➤ Sean Connery, Gert Fröbe and Harold Sakata at Pinewood's Fort Knox set.

▲ (And following pages) Sean Connery under the watchful eye of Honor Blackman and her subordinates.

▲ (And following spread) *Goldfinger* director Guy Hamilton oversees the rehearsal of Bond and Oddjob's fight scene.

◄ Sean Connery enjoys a rare moment to himself.

▲ Sean Connery handcuffed to a nuclear bomb in the Fort Knox vault set at Pinewood.

◄▲ Sean Connery and Honor Blackman in a playful mood as they film the final scene of *Goldfinger*.

▲ Honor Blackman arrives at the premiere of *Goldfinger* wearing a gold finger of her own.

▲ (And following pages) Sean Connery and Luciana Paluzzi pose in bed for photographers.

◄   Sean Connery and Luciana Paluzzi (Fiona Volpe) share a joke on the set of *Thunderball*.

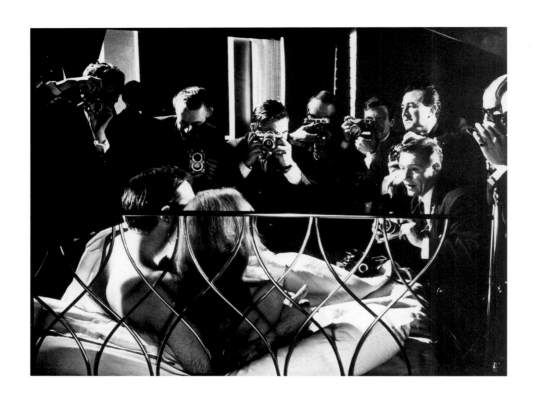

➤ Sean Connery and Claudine Auger (Domino) during a promotional interview for *Thunderball* with *Daily Mirror* reporter Donald Zec.

◀ (And following pages) Sean Connery enjoying some Japanese hospitality during the filming of *You Only Live Twice* at Pinewood in July 1966.

▲ Actress Karin Dor (Helga Brandt) looks on nervously as she prepares to take a dive in the piranha pool.

▲ Karin Dor and director Lewis Gilbert watch on as stuntwoman Jenny Le Fre prepares to fall into the pool.

▲ (And following page) Sean Connery in bed with actress Akiko Wakabayashi during the filming of *You Only Live Twice*.

◄ Karin Dor takes the plunge.

▲ Aerial view of production designer Ken Adam's extraordinary volcano lair set at Pinewood Studios for *You Only Live Twice*.

◄ Inside the volcano lair at Pinewood Studios.

▲ Sean Connery and his *You Only Live Twice* co-stars. Left to right: Lois Maxwell (Miss Moneypenny), Akiko Wakabayashi (Aki), Karin Dor (Helga Brandt) and Mie Hama (Kissy Suzuki).

⌃ (And following page) England's 1966 World Cup football squad take a break from the tournament to visit Pinewood Studios during the filming of *You Only Live Twice*.

∧ (And following page) George Lazenby and Diana Rigg filming
On Her Majesty's Secret Service's casino scene.

∧ (And following pages) George Lazenby happily plays up for photographers as he prepares to film a scene outside the College of Arms in the City of London.

⌃ (And previous pages) George Lazenby and Diana Rigg filming a scene in Switzerland.

◀▲ (And following pages) Shooting the wedding sequence of *On Her Majesty's Secret Service* in Estoril, Portugal.

▲ Roger Moore is unveiled as the new James Bond by producers Harry Saltzman and Cubby Broccoli.

➤ Jane Seymour (Solitaire) in her extraordinary costume for *Live and Let Die*.

▲➤ Roger Moore and Jane Seymour film *Live and Let Die*'s voodoo ceremony sequence at Pinewood Studios.

▲ *The Man with the Golden Gun* stars Britt Ekland (Mary Goodnight), Maud Adams (Andrea Anders) and Hervé Villechaize (Nick Nack) at the film's premiere in 1974.

▼ Roger Moore and his wife, Luisa Mattioli, at the premiere of *The Man with the Golden Gun*.

▲ Roger Moore greets Prince Phillip as his co-star Christopher Lee (Francisco Scaramanga) and wife Luisa Mattioli look on.

▲ Several of the 'Bond girls' from *The Spy Who Loved Me* pose with 007's Lotus Esprit.

◄▲ Roger Moore and Barbara Bach (Anya Amasova) greet Prime Minister Harold Wilson when he visits Pinewood Studios to officially open the largest film stage in the world on 5 December 1976. The supertanker set was designed by Ken Adam for *The Spy Who Loved Me*.

◀ (And following pages) Roger Moore pictured with his *Moonraker* co-star Lois Chiles (Holly Goodhead) at a photocall in Paris prior to filming.

▲ A photocall for *For Your Eyes Only* in London, 23 June 1981.
Roger Moore poses with several of the film's 'Bond girls'.

▲ Roger Moore and his co-star Maud Adams (Octopussy) at a photocall for *Octopussy* in 1983.

◄ Roger Moore and his *Octopussy* 'Bond girls' pictured here at a photocall in London on 1 June 1983.

➤ Roger Moore with 'Bond girls' Mary Stavin (left) and Carolyn Seward (right) filming *Octopussy* at RAF Upper Heyford in Oxfordshire.

▲➤ Roger Moore with his son, Geoffrey, at the RAF Upper Heyford location on 23 August 1982.

▲ The reopening of the world's largest film stage at Pinewood Studios after it was destroyed by a fire. Roger Moore is pictured in January 1985 with producer Cubby Broccoli and co-stars (left to right) Fiona Fullerton (Pola Ivanova), Tanya Roberts (Stacey Sutton), Alison Doody (Jenny Flex) and Christopher Walken (Max Zorin) during the production of *A View to a Kill*.

▲ Tanya Roberts and Grace Jones (May Day) pose for photographers at *A View to a Kill* photocall.

▲ Roger Moore and Christopher Walken share a joke in between takes on *A View to a Kill*.

◄ Roger Moore with Alison Doody, Tanya Roberts and Fiona Fullerton.

▲➤ A tough new Bond also shows his brighter side. Timothy Dalton filming *The Living Daylights* in Gibraltar on 3 October 1986.